After Miscarriage
A Journey to Healing

Lori B. Leo

Hingham House Publishing
Hanover, Massachusetts

Information contained in this book is not intended as a substitute for medical advice or attention. Please consult your doctor or health care provider for individual professional care. References are provided for informational purposes only and do not constitute endorsement of any websites or other sources. Readers should be aware that the websites listed in this book might change.

Cover design: Sarah Cotur
Interior design and layout: Glenna Collett
Cover photograph: Roger Pellissier

ISBN 9781483584317 (pbk.)
ISBN 9781483584324 (ebook)

Library of Congress Control Number 2016917705

Printed in the United States of America

Hingham House Publishing
www.lorileoauthor.com

*To Harrison, my precious son, you are and
will always be my most treasured gift.
I am immeasurably blessed to be your mother.*

*To all my babies and all the babies lost through miscarriage,
we love you . . . .*

Contents

Acknowledgments

Six years ago I embarked on this journey and I am grateful that life always interrupted the completion of my book. For years I was drawn back to one of the most painful yet rewarding experiences in my life. As I read, edited and reread during this cathartic process, I was still brought to tears. Although time has helped to heal the emotional suffering from multiple miscarriages, there are moments from those two years that will forever be indelible.

I must thank you all for your patience during the dormant phases of this book. Sarah Cotur, when you read my manuscript and said you could not put it down, you gave me hope. You fulfilled every wish for the cover design. Roger Pellissier, thank you for the beautiful photo you took of our family. You are a gifted photographer. To my editor, Marti Dryk, many thanks for your enthusiasm and faith in this book. Our many conversations encouraged me. To Glenna Collett, thank you for your guidance and wisdom.

To my parents who taught me to
never give up
be the best person you can
do the best job possible no matter what you do in life
pick yourself up by the bootstraps when you are down
and move forward.

Leisa, a friend like you is found once in a lifetime for the lucky few. Although you are no longer here to see this book to completion, your friendship, encouraging words, prayers, hugs and endless support will never be forgotten. You were always by my side and are missed far beyond description. To my precious friend Kris for your endless prayers and the impeccable timing of your telephone calls that came when I needed them the most.

Mike, my husband and best friend . . . I can never adequately thank you for never saying no.

And to Harrison, this journey would have never been complete without you.

Introduction

Miscarriage is the Silent Loss. It's the Hidden Grief. Talk shows don't discuss "recovering" from a miscarriage. It's rarely written about in women's magazines, and few churches have ministries that reach out to women who have suffered an early pregnancy loss.

When I mentioned to a friend who works in publishing that I was writing a book on miscarriage, she told me it would be a "brown bag book"—a reference to the days before online bookstores when a shopper would ask that an embarrassing purchase be quickly stuffed inside a brown paper bag. It would, she said, be a book that women might not purchase in a store simply because they were too self-conscious to hand it over the counter to a sales clerk. That "brown bag" feeling was something I understood all too well. While you can't turn on the television without seeing an endless stream of people sharing the most sordid and intimate details of their lives, miscarriage is still hidden in the shadows. I suffered four miscarriages in two years, and during that time I knew no one who had experienced a miscarriage, or so I thought. It was only later when I began to speak openly about my loss, that I discovered how many of my friends and acquaintances had, like me, struggled in silence with their grief.

According to the American Pregnancy Association, studies reveal that anywhere from 10-25% of all clinically recognized pregnancies will end in miscarriage. We still don't talk about it. How crazy is that?

I was very fortunate. After my last miscarriage, I finally found the help I needed when I joined a support group and began working with a therapist. This was a huge step for me because I always thought of myself as someone who could handle any problems in my life. As I began to reach out and speak about my experiences with miscarrying, I found that many women still have nowhere to turn, no one with whom to share their story, and no one to help them navigate the turbulent emotional waters that follow a miscarriage.

How do you cope when your best friend becomes pregnant? How do you respond to hurtful comments such as, "It's a blessing"? "Who knows what might have been wrong with your baby?" What's the best way to find a miscarriage support group that's right for you? How can family and friends offer the support you really need?

My hope is that this book will go beyond bringing the comfort that comes from a shared experience by offering practical and prayerful guidance to parents, as well as their families and friends, as they begin the journey to healing.

Lori's Story

1

"I'm Pregnant!"

I got pregnant on our honeymoon. I'd waited thirty-six years to find my soul mate, and I wanted to celebrate with a once in a lifetime honeymoon. Mike and I decided we would spend ten days driving around France, beginning in Normandy, then down through the Champagne region and finally south to the famous sunny beaches of the Cote d'Azur. We made no hotel reservations, simply stopping in a village at the end of the day and checking into the local hotels (sometimes a great idea and sometimes not so great). We toured vineyards, raced at a go-cart track outside St. Tropez and we ate ham and cheese sandwiches on buttery baguettes, olives soaked in Herbs de Provence, cheese that Mike likened to the smell of his socks at the end of a long day, and the best herb roasted chicken I've ever tasted that had been purchased at a tiny gas station outside Lyon.

Although Mike and I had talked about starting a family, it had always been in a when-it-happens-it-happens sort of way. Little did we know that "it" was about to happen.

After we had returned from our honeymoon in June 2000, I went back to work as a chemical engineer doing health and safety inspections for the State of Massachusetts. Mike came to live with me in the small two-bedroom home outside of Boston that had belonged to my great-Aunt Fran. When she was dying of cancer, my parents and I had moved in and lived with her for two months, taking turns watching over her. I slept in a tiny den just off the living room where Aunt Fran was confined to a hospital bed and at night, I could hear her air mattress going chhhhh chhhhh as she turned herself to try to ease the pain. One night I awoke at two in the morning to the sounds of her groaning. I got up and came to sit next to her bed. She was a woman of great faith. When she began talking, it felt as if she were getting her words straight from God. I held her hand as she struggled to speak through the pain.

"You're going to have a child, and you're going to have a little boy," she whispered.

I was in my late twenties, not yet thinking about marriage or children, but I put her words away in my heart, not realizing how prophetic her words would be.

In early July, my period was late. At first I didn't think much about it, and I didn't even tell Mike, because after all, who gets pregnant on their honeymoon? When my period still hadn't arrived after a week, I decided to stop at a pharmacy on my way home from work and pick up a pregnancy test. I found myself standing in a brightly lit aisle utterly bewildered by the dozens of choices. Then I saw a brand with a two pack and grabbed it. That was the engineer in me—never rely on the results of just one test. At that time, you were only supposed to do the test first thing in the morning, but I couldn't wait. As soon as I got home I ripped open the package and raced to the bathroom.

Sure enough, it was positive. I remember sitting on the bed looking down at the pink line on the stick and thinking, *Oh, my gosh. I'm really pregnant.* I think I was excited and stunned all at the same time. I had hoped to surprise Mike with pink and blue balloons, but there was no time. When he arrived home, I just blurted it out.

"I'm pregnant," I announced, holding up the stick with a faint pink line.

In our home, my husband is known as The Voice of Reason and this time was no exception.

"These tests aren't always accurate," cautioned Mike, "why don't you do another one in the morning just to make sure?"

He was right, I thought. More people than I could remember had warned me that I'd have a hard time conceiving at thirty-six. What were the odds, I thought, that I would find myself pregnant just weeks after my wedding? The sun was barely up the next morning when I took the test again. Another pink line. I really was pregnant. Or as Mike would say when he began telling everyone he knew,

"Lori has a bun in the oven."

The first person I called was my mother. As all the friends and family who have been jolted out of a sound sleep by one of my "I didn't wake you did I?" phone calls will tell you, I am a really early riser. On this day, I managed to wait until the very reasonable hour of 6:30 a.m. to phone her.

"I'm pregnant!"

Once my mother got over the shock of being awakened with this unexpected news, she was thrilled.

"Oh, honey, I'm so glad for you."

I could hear my father in the background and then my mother telling him,

"It's Lori—she's pregnant!"

My mother is also a voice of reason, and before we hung up, she reminded me to take care of myself and not overdo it. She knew both my sister and I have the tendency to push hard and do everything full out no matter our condition, a tendency I have to say we inherited from both our parents.

Next to get the good news were my sister, Lisa and my best friend, who is also somewhat confusingly named Leisa. When I began telling close friends and family, there were some of the expected jokes about "maybe it was all that French food," but I could see they were all happy for me. While many of my friends had waited until the end of their first trimester to announce their pregnancies, I had no hesitation about telling people closest to me, even at this early stage. After all, I was healthy, I exercised and I ate well. What could happen?

As most newly pregnant women will tell you, the world suddenly seems filled to overflowing with other pregnant women and babies. When I'd pass a woman with a baby in a stroller, I'd smile and nod as if we were all members of an exclusive club. If I went to a department store to buy a shirt for Mike, I'd end up in the baby section looking at tiny little dresses and pants.

My mother bought me a stroller and her friend Mary, an extraordinary woman who earned a Bachelor of Arts degree from Harvard at age eighty-nine, crocheted a beautiful sea-foam green, baby blue and white afghan for me. It was a treasured gift I would keep tucked away in a drawer until I was finally, many years later, able to use it in my son's stroller. I went to Whole Foods, bought an enormous bottle of prenatal vitamins and called to make an appointment with an OB/GYN at one of Boston's most famous hospitals. Like everything else in my life, I was going to make certain my pregnancy was well-organized and under control.

I had always been an athlete (I lifted weights, ran, skied downhill and cross country, and rode horses), but when I became pregnant, I switched into high gear and became even more disciplined about my workout routine and what I ate. I continued to run, work out with weights, and became obsessed with the health benefits of juicing. Every morning I "juiced" a big thermos of carrot-apple-ginger juice to take to work. I thought I was doing everything I needed to do to ensure we had a healthy baby.

In August, I was nearing the end of my first trimester, and we seemed headed toward an uneventful and successful pregnancy. Then early one Friday afternoon, I went to the ladies room at my office and discovered small spots of blood on my underwear. My first reaction was disbelief. I began feeling faint and short of breath as if I might start hyperventilating. My chest tightened as I managed to walk back to my cubicle and sat there staring at my blinking computer screen. What should I do? I had no idea and that in itself was terrifying. I'd always been a problem solver but this time I felt absolutely adrift. I called my sister, Lisa. *She has three children. She must know what's happening to me.*

"What's does spotting like this mean?" I asked her, my voice almost a whisper.

Office cubicles don't make for private conversations, and this was one call I didn't want everyone overhearing. When Lisa responded, her voice was unexpectedly quiet and deliberate, and I could tell she was trying not to frighten me.

"It could be the beginning of a miscarriage, but it could just as easily be spotting that's totally normal. Have you called your doctor?"

Not before I call Mike and quickly dialed his office. Mike tried his very best to be reassuring in spite of the rising panic he could hear in my voice.

"Don't worry. This happens to some women and they go on to have a normal pregnancy. Call the doctor and let them know what's happening—and try to relax. Just take it one step at a time."

When I finally made the call to my doctor's office, my hands were shaking so badly I almost dropped the phone. I remember thinking that the woman who answered sounded so calm and I realized she must get frantic calls from pregnant women all the time. It had seemed like days before my doctor called back, but it was less than an hour. I spent that hour online at the State of Massachusetts' computer researching miscarriages. This was something that was truly foolish, as each situation is unique, and all it did was make me think I must have done something that could be causing a miscarriage.

When I did speak to the doctor, the only thing she told me was, "There could be a threat of a miscarriage."

We would have to wait and see what happened over the next few days. A few days, I thought, *Who could bear to wait that long?*

As the day went on the spotting never stopped and I could feel my world crumbling around me. I tried to work, but focusing on a pile of health and safety inspections was an impossibility. At 3:00 p.m. I left for home without telling anyone in the office what was happening. On the drive home, I called my mother. Just hearing her voice gave me such comfort. As I got out of the car and walked past the red roses climbing over the picket fence surrounding our house, all I could think was, *You can't be having a miscarriage. No one who lives in a house with roses and a white picket fence can lose a child.*

When I saw Mike, I just melted into his arms. For a moment, I seemed to imagine we were back in St. Tropez, spending a lazy, carefree afternoon on the beach. As I let go of Mike, reality took what felt like a death grip on my heart—I was in our house in Boston not in France, and I might be losing our child. For some reason, I remembered the evangelist Benny Hinn was holding a healing service that evening in Worcester, a town about an hour away.

"I need to go to Worcester," I blurted out to a bewildered Mike. "Benny Hinn will pray for me and everything will be all right."

Before Mike knew what was happening, I had grabbed my car keys and was heading out the door. Mike was extremely patient and understanding; he didn't try to talk me out of it. He just took the car keys from my hand and started to drive toward Worcester. When we got to the arena the first thing I saw was a "Sold Out" sign in the box office window. At this point, it had been eight years since I'd accepted Jesus as my Savior but it had been eight years of taking tiny steps toward a relationship with the Lord. This was the first big crisis of faith in my life since becoming a believer, and when it hit, I realized I had no foundation on which to stand. Instead of going to prayer, I began to sob, and my body started to shake with fear.

Mike turned the car around and told me we were going to my parent's cottage on Cape Cod. Until the diversion to Worcester, we'd intended to drive out and spend a leisurely weekend with them. I paged the doctor again on the ride down but got the same wait and see response. When I insisted she give me a better answer, she paused for a moment and then told me,

"If the blood turns bright red it might mean you're losing the baby."

2

Empty Handed and Brokenhearted

When we arrived at my parent's house, we parked next to the pink hydrangeas that lined the fence along the driveway. We had used pots of hydrangeas as center-pieces at our wedding reception and my mother, who couldn't bear the thought of such beautiful plants being thrown out, had rescued them and brought them home. When I saw that sea of pink, all I could think of was how hopeful and joyful I had been on that day; how certain I'd been of spending a long happy life with Mike and our children.

As we walked in the front door, I could smell garlic, a sure sign my father was busy in the kitchen preparing a big pot of red sauce for that evening's pasta dinner.

My mother was setting the table in the dining room, and when she saw me, she pulled me into her arms and whispered, "Don't worry. Everything will be all right."

Oh, please God, I thought. *Let that be true.*

At dinner I was in a fog, staring out the bay window that overlooks the ocean and paying no attention to the conversation or any attempts to lift my spirits. My mind was racing as I thought back to a sharp pain I'd felt four weeks ago when Mike and I were in Maine on a biking trip. We were having dinner at a restaurant in Cape Neddick when I felt an intense pain in my stomach; the kind that makes you stop breathing for a few seconds. I'd dismissed it then, but *What if I'd pushed myself too hard by biking uphill without changing gears? What about all the nights I'd spent weight lifting at the gym during the last few months. Had I done something reckless that might be causing a miscarriage?*

Saturday afternoon friends came and went, as they always did in my parent's neighborhood—dropping by to sit on mismatched patio chairs in the yard, drinking ice tea or wine and sharing the neighborhood goings on. I recall telling a few people what was happening and while everyone was very kind no one said, "That happened to me" or "Don't worry, that happened to me and I was fine." I felt absolutely and totally alone.

Late Saturday afternoon the spotting turned to red blood and the hope I had been holding onto so tightly cracked, crumbled, and shattered. My breath became short, labored, and I felt as if I was being suffocated by the reality of what was to come.

By the time we sat down at the table for dinner, my sister Lisa had arrived with her husband and children. I couldn't eat. I couldn't even swallow. Conversation at my parent's dinner table is always lively, loud, and happily chaotic. Tonight I was barely listening until my brother-in-law began describing in detail the birth of my youngest niece. I felt the room spinning around me as if I was in a boxing match and slowly being knocked down by jab after jab to my heart.

My father told everyone to change the subject. I grabbed a glass of wine (*What did it matter now?*), went outside and sat on a lounge chair. I wanted no one near me. Maybe I was selfish to think that what I was going through wasn't as important to Mike, but that's how I felt at the time. It was as if I'd been thrown into a swimming pool, found myself desperately struggling to get to the surface and gasping for just enough air to survive a moment longer.

Later that night the pain started. It felt like contractions, and it kept intensifying. Finally, I couldn't tolerate the pain any longer. Just before two in the morning, I woke Mike up and told him he had to take me to the hospital. It was a small community hospital, but it did have an ER. They took me right into an examining room, started an IV and gave me Demerol for the pain. I looked at the nurse, and I asked her if I was going to die—I was that scared.

She patted my hand, told me, "Oh, no dear," and covered me up with warm blankets.

I could see someone from admissions standing with Mike and asking him questions like "What's her date of birth?" Mike was so upset he couldn't remember my birth-day or even how to spell my name. I had to answer the questions on the admissions form.

The doctor on call was very young and Mike told me later he had seen him at the nurse's station looking through what seemed to be a thick medical textbook—and he was reading the section on miscarriage. What he read must have made him realize that my case was beyond his level of training because he called in an OB/GYN. It couldn't have been more than twenty minutes before she came, but it seemed like an eternity. She gave me an ultrasound that confirmed my worst nightmare. We had, she told us, lost the baby at eight weeks and I was now miscarrying at twelve weeks.

It was all over in another twenty minutes. The doctor took the baby and put him (. . . *or was it her? We never knew.*) into a glass jar sitting on a metal cart. She rolled the cart out of the room, and that was the last I saw of my baby. It was over, and I was no longer pregnant. There was no lon-ger life inside me. I left the hospital empty handed and broken hearted.

The peace of dawn was breaking as we arrived back at my parent's cottage. Dawn has always been my favorite time of the day—the hustle and bustle of the world was still under cover. You can feel the peace of God and be present with Him. The verse from Psalm 46, "Be still and know that I am God," began running over and over again in my mind. I was so emotionally exhausted I couldn't find the energy to walk the extra steps to our bedroom. I laid down on the couch in the living room and fell asleep to the sounds of the waves crashing against the rocks.

Monday morning I called into work and tried to keep my voice steady. As I told the secretary who answered the phone that I had suffered a miscarriage and would be taking a few days off, she was so kind and said exactly the right thing—a simple "I'm so sorry, Lori."

Mike wasn't able to take time off to stay home with me. I decided to spend the next few days on the Cape with my parents, who were and always have been my greatest support.

On Tuesday morning, my mother came into my room, sat down on the edge of the bed and told me something so precious. She'd awakened in the middle of the night to the overpowering smell of roses. The scent seemed to be coming from outside. She sat up in bed and looked out the window. There, standing on the darkened lawn, she saw Our Lord Jesus holding a tiny baby. I broke down in tears when she told me, but I was comforted. I knew that the Lord was taking care of my child and that one day we would be reunited.

3

Dents along the Road

Three weeks after my first miscarriage, I found myself standing—sobbing and alone—on the shoulder of the Braintree Expressway outside of Boston. Well, not exactly alone. A man was shouting obscenities at the top of his lungs and was racing toward me.

The day was already a miserable one. Thirty minutes earlier I'd given away Tawny, the horse Mike had bought me shortly before we were married. She was an off-the-track Thoroughbred, and I had reluctantly decided she was too hot for me to handle safely, particularly if I would become pregnant again. I'd found her a wonderful home with Debbie, a woman from Maine. She'd met me that afternoon at the barn where I boarded Tawny. After we'd loaded Tawny onto her trailer, Debbie followed me out to the Expressway. As we came to the split where you go left to Boston or right to Cape Cod, I waved out the window to remind her to go toward Boston. As I was waving, my wedding ring went flying off into three lanes of rush hour traffic.

I hit my brakes and, without thinking about the cars that were hurtling toward me, careened over into the breakdown lane. By the absolute grace of God, I didn't cause a major pile-up. One man was angry enough at what I'd done that he pulled over in front of me, got out of his car like a lunatic, yelling and swearing at me. I remember thinking he looked exactly like one of those crazed fans that scream non-stop at hockey games and wish they could get onto the ice and be part of the fights.

At this point I was literally shell-shocked—I'd miscarried my baby, given up my horse, lost my wedding ring, and now I had this manic screaming at me. I had nothing left. I could not even summon a response to his tirade. I silently cried out to God.

"How much more can you expect me to take? How many more tests must I endure?"

Then God sent me a wonderful angel. She was an angel disguised as a thin brunette woman in her forties wearing a nondescript pair of dark brown pants and a tan sweater. She and her teenage daughter had been driving in a car behind me. When she saw what was happening, she'd pulled over to make certain I was all right. Without saying a word, she walked over and quietly put herself between me and the raging man. When she looked at me, her face was so gentle and kind I found myself blurting out everything to her—the miscarriage, the wedding ring and now all this. When I finished, she turned to the man, who had literally been struck silent by her arrival and my avalanche of words and told him very matter-of-factly that she'd called the police even though no cars had been hit or damaged. There was no reason for him to be there. Miraculously, he turned around and left.

By now, I was freezing cold, shaking from the shock and desperately trying to figure out if there was any way I would ever be able to recover my wedding ring. For one reckless moment, I gazed at the three lanes of cars flying by at 70 miles per hour and wondered how foolish it would be to run out into traffic and look for my ring.

I went to get a sweater out of my car. As I opened the passenger door I looked down. Sitting on the ground next to the car was my wedding ring. Not in the middle of the highway being run over by semis and tractor-trailers, but safely on the grass beside my car. Just two feet more and it would have rolled over an embankment and been lost forever.

I started to cry—not just tears of joy, but also tears for everything I'd been through that day. Then tears of relief and comfort because I knew God had been with me. He had shown Himself to me in the most visible tangible way. I had been so overwhelmed by my grief in the weeks since my miscarriage that it took something like this to get my attention; to remind me that He cared for me and would never forsake me.

The woman—I'm afraid I have to call her that, because in all the chaos, I never asked her name—came over, and I showed her the ring. I'm sure I must have been babbling about it being a miracle and making no sense at all, but she smiled, hugged me and told me I needed to go home. There had been no harm done to anyone, and she would deal with the police when they arrived. As I drove off, I turned to wave a final thank you—but she was no longer there.

My wedding ring has a few dents in it, but I treasure each of them as a reminder of that day. Hebrews 12:1 promises believers that we are, "Surrounded by such a great cloud of witnesses," men and women of great faith who came before us. I often think of my ring as a cloud of witness. I'll look down at it when I'm making dinner, grooming a horse or holding my son, and I know that God is always with me—even in the darkest of times.

4

"Wait a Few Days and Check Again . . ."

Life, somewhat to my surprise, did go on after my first miscarriage. I woke up every morning, drove to my office in Boston, met with clients and continued to work on my assigned projects. I leased a new horse, the quiet and steady Noble, and went riding with my best friend, Leisa. Mike and I went out to dinner with Leisa and her boyfriend and enjoyed time with my sister and her family. There was always a constant tugging at my emotions. A day never went by when I didn't think about the baby I had lost.

I became a pro at hiding those unsettling emotions. To my friends and family, I had always been Lori the Rock, the shoulder to lean on, the sounding board. If anyone had a crisis or a problem, I was the one who would calmly and efficiently get it solved. I was so rooted in my old identity as "the strong one" that I didn't tell anyone, even Mike, about the overwhelming emotional darkness that began to envelop me.

My tightly controlled emotional world began to unravel once the Christmas season came—the time when I would have been close to delivering our baby. I did manage to muster up enough holiday spirit to go with Mike to pick out a tree and set it up in our living room, but I decorated it without the joy I had always taken in the season. I don't know if everyone was trying to be sensitive to the timing or simply thought I had "gotten over it," but no one made any mention of the baby. That was a lethal wound to my heart.

While I was well aware of the despair and unhappiness I carried with me each day, what I hadn't yet confronted was the enormous streak of bitterness that was slowly eating away at my soul. The bitterness surfaced one evening just before Christmas when I went to dinner at a local restaurant with my mother. When we walked in, I saw that the hostess, a tall, dark-haired young woman in her early thirties, was heavily pregnant. I suddenly found myself literally hating the very sight of her. *How could she have the nerve to walk in front of me looking so blissfully pregnant?*

As my mother and I sat on a bench waiting for our table, I let loose my anger.

"Doesn't she understand what a loss I've suffered? How dare she parade herself around when I'm in such pain?"

My mother was justifiably horrified by my outburst. Since I was obviously irrational, she was smart enough not to add to the conversation and sat quietly while I continued to focus my wrath on the innocent young hostess. By the time she came over to show us to our table, I had managed to control my rage but I stared daggers at her as she seated us. I still feel guilty about my behavior that evening. It was the first time I realized how deep and destructive my anger over the miscarriage had become.

Christmas that year brought both comfort and pain. The service at church on Christmas Eve was exactly what I needed. The dim lights and the familiar and soothing music of Christmas hymns gave me solace. In the months since my miscarriage, I had found that only God could provide the comfort and peace I so desperately sought. I finally realized after all these years that true peace and comfort only come from God. Mike and I had started attending a home group. We would meet weekly in the evening with four or five other couples from our church. There would be time for Bible study and then time to pray for one another. I also joined a women's Bible study with Leisa. The prayers of my church family were what sustained me.

That evening, there was an altar call for anyone who wished the elders to pray for them and both Mike and I walked forward. Our request was simple "for a child" and their prayers helped me gather my strength for what was about to come later that evening at my parent's home.

Every year, my parents hosted a traditional Italian Christmas Eve dinner that's known as the Feast of the Seven Fishes. My mother would be busy almost a week before preparing the house for the many guests. My father would spend an entire day and night barricaded in the kitchen preparing fried calamari, shrimp scampi, anchovies wrapped in pizza dough and Seafood Fra Diavolo over homemade macaroni. When I say a large group turned up for dinner, I mean really large. It wasn't unusual for fifty aunts, uncles, cousins and family friends to stop by throughout the course of the night. It was always a high-spirited and joyous evening—the conversation was so loud the noise level rivaled a rock concert—and it wasn't unheard of for dessert to be served at midnight.

As with most large families, whenever we get together, much of the talk revolves around children—"Look how he's grown" or "What grade is she in now?" That year, I was the proverbial elephant in the room, and as I moved from group to group, I desperately wanted someone to ask me how I was doing. No one, with the exception of my cousin Nancy, brought up the forbidden subject. Nancy was undergoing fertility treatments (another forbidden topic). The two of us stood in the dining room, surround by a mob of laughing family, talking about our struggles to have a child. At that time, I didn't know anyone else who shared that struggle and even the brief time I spent with Nancy that evening helped me to understand that I wasn't alone.

Christmas day that year was especially hard. My mother got up early and headed to my sister's house to watch the kid's expressions as they ripped open the presents Santa had left under the tree while my father stayed home to begin making the antipasto and cooking pizzelles (an Italian cookie) that he'd bring to dinner at my sister's home. Me? I was waking at the crack of dawn, feeling overwhelmed by my sense of loss. Mike made a special effort that morning to raise my spirits, knowing that instead of arriving at Christmas dinner seven months pregnant and glowing, I was instead dreading the prospect of watching my nieces and nephew open the gifts my parents would bring over for them. It was a day when all I hoped to do was hide my despair.

After Christmas, I felt as if my only focus was trying to get pregnant. It must have been the magic of the holidays or the long, cold winter, but in January I was a day late. While a day may seem like nothing to most women, it was enough for me to break out my stash of pregnancy kits—I should have bought stock in the company I had so many on hand! This time I followed the instructions to the letter and waited until the next morning to do the test. At first light, I snuck into the bathroom and impatiently waited the three minutes, hoping and praying to see a pink line. I was ecstatic when one faintly appeared and woke Mike up to tell him the news.

"Wait a few days and check again," he cautioned, not wanting me to get my hopes up.

Undeterred, I returned to the bathroom and took another test. In three minutes, I was back in the bedroom.

"It's real," I said, holding out the stick with the pink line. "Two tests can't be wrong."

"Wait and check again in a few days," said Mike.

I immediately discounted what he said. I knew I was pregnant. It was the first time in six months that I felt my spirits lift.

I reconfirmed it a few days later (all those test kits came in handy) and called my OB/GYN to let him know I was pregnant. I scheduled my first appointment, but I never even made it into the office. I was working from home one afternoon when I began to feel as if I was getting my period. I flew upstairs to the bathroom and saw I was beginning to hemorrhage. When I called my doctor's office, they told me to get to an emergency room as soon as possible. Mike, who thankfully was home that afternoon, got me into the car and tightly held my hand as we drove in silence the fifteen minutes it took to reach the ER.

Luckily, I was seen by a nurse-midwife who was truly an angel sent by God. When the ultrasound confirmed that I had suffered a second miscarriage, she wrapped her arms around me and held me while I sobbed. That was all she needed to do. Her arms brought such comfort; it was as if I had my mother beside me.

A week later, I went with my sister and two nieces to Logan Airport to pick up my parents, who had been on vacation in Florida. The minute I saw them coming down the escalator to the baggage claim area, I broke into a flood of tears.

My mother came over, held me close and once again assured me, "Oh, honey, everything will be all right."

My mother is one of those people who always looks for the silver lining. Not in a naive saccharine sweet way, but as a woman of faith who knows that "all things work together for good to those that believe and are called according to His will" (Romans 8:28). Growing up, she'd always tell me, "Have faith, Lori, things will work out." That's how she's lived her life, always looking forward to the happiness up ahead. That day, I clung tightly to her bright vision of my future.

5

"There's No Heartbeat"

After a third miscarriage, my GYN had referred me to an OB/GYN who specialized in multiple miscarriages. He was incredibly kind, always taking the time to talk with me and patiently answer my constant stream of questions. After several visits and multiple tests and procedures, it was decided that there was nothing "wrong" with me. I was now in a category of miscarriages they called "unexplained losses."

At the end of December 2001, I became pregnant for the fourth time. I think my friends and family would all agree that it probably saved my sanity, as I was obsessed with becoming pregnant again. My world revolved around the ovulation testing kit. I lived from one period to the next. Sex became almost like a second job—mechanical and brought little joy.

When I called the specialist's office to tell them I was pregnant, they told me the doctor I liked so very much had left the hospital to join a practice that dealt only with fertility issues. Since becoming pregnant had never been my problem, I was sadly unable to follow him and the office assigned my case to another physician in the practice. During our first appointment, he reviewed my records, confirmed that I was now a "high-risk" patient and ended our conversation with the words, "If you're going to have another miscarriage, there's nothing I can do about it."

I was speechless. *You insensitive idiot.* I thought. *Knowing my history, how could you even make a comment such as that!*

I left the office and never returned. The next day I called the hospital where the practice was located and lodged a complaint with Patient Relations. Perhaps he'd think twice before ever again being so thoughtless and cruel.

As a high-risk patient I knew it was essential that someone continually monitor my pregnancy, so I asked my GYN to manage all my prenatal care. I was so thankful he agreed to do so. At six weeks, he sent me to an ultrasound center to check for a heartbeat and to make certain the baby's development was on schedule. Everything was positive with a strong heartbeat and good progesterone levels. I was elated and confident that this time I would give birth to a happy, healthy baby—a confidence I shared with all my family and friends.

My GYN had scheduled a second ultrasound at eight weeks. When the day arrived, I set off for the center so certain everything would be okay that I even drove myself. After the tech had completed the ultrasound, she told me I might not be far enough along, and they would have to do it again vaginally. I started to become concerned because during the first ultrasound no one had seemed at all worried about my not being far enough along. When I asked the tech if everything was okay, she gave me one of those "If I smile she'll think everything is fine" smiles and told me she'd be right back with a radiologist. I was now truly terrified and began crying out to God, *This can't be happening to me again. Please let them find a strong heartbeat. Please let them find a strong heartbeat.*

The radiologist came in and without even introducing himself, turned and looked at the monitor. He stared at it for a moment and then, in an icy voice devoid of any compassion, told me, "There's no heartbeat."

He didn't say I'm sorry. He simply walked out of the room. I put my head between my knees and started sobbing.

The tech tried to console me, but I couldn't stop crying. I don't know that I've ever felt a pain that deep or agonizing. Another woman came in and gathered up my clothes from a chair in the corner and told me I needed to get dressed. She tried to offer some consoling words, but I couldn't hear them through my pain. A few minutes later, the tech walked me out of the room and took me out some back way. I didn't have to go through the waiting room and look at all the pregnant women. In one way, this was a kind gesture, but in another way it made me feel as if I was a diseased person that needed to be shuffled out the back.

When I got to the parking garage, I had a moment of panic because I wasn't sure I could remember where I'd parked. Once I did find my car, all I could do for what seemed like hours was sit behind the wheel and sob. I finally managed to start the car and back out of the space, but I was still sobbing so uncontrollably that my body was almost convulsing. When I stopped to pay the parking attendant, his eyes got very wide, and he asked, "Ma'am, are you okay?"

He must have thought I'd been told that I had a terminal illness. I couldn't even respond. I simply handed him the money and drove out of the garage.

A few blocks later, I pulled over to the side of the road and tried to stop crying long enough to call Mike. I knew he was waiting to hear how the ultrasound had gone, and I didn't know how I would tell him the news. I could hear the terrible sorrow in his voice, and for the first time I felt a crack in the emotional fortress he had built to support me. Mike met me at home. I was so grateful he didn't fall back on all those clichés about "we can try again." He simply put his arms around me and held me tightly.

Thankfully, in the years since my first miscarriage, my relationship with God had grown strong. I'd become involved in women's Bible studies at church and begun to share with the other women my struggles to have a child.

That evening, a new study, one I was looking forward to, was beginning at church. Even though I'd managed to stop crying, I was still utterly distraught and considered not going. Leisa, my most beloved prayer partner, urged me to go. I knew I could find no greater comfort than being surrounded by the women who had so prayerfully supported me. On the drive to the church, as I was pleading to God for some relief and comfort from this emotional turmoil, I was suddenly struck by the beauty of the night—crisp air and a dark blue sky filled with what seemed like thousands of stars.

The plan for that evening's study had been to watch a short film from Beth Moore's *Living Proof Ministries*, but just as the film began, the power went out on a cloudless night with no rain. After a few minutes of sitting in darkness, the woman leading the group stood up and suggested we use the time to pray for one another and asked for requests as to who needed specific prayer. As we stood in a large circle holding hands, I struggled to get the words out.

"I'm about to lose my fourth pregnancy," I stuttered.

I could hear an intake of breath from friends in the group and see the sorrow written on their faces. As everyone gathered around me and began to pray, it felt as if God had sent not just someone, but an army of prayer warriors to sustain me.

I had decided I didn't want the baby to come into the world by a D & C, that I would wait for God's time and allow a natural miscarriage. In the four weeks I waited, it

was the prayers of the women in my Bible study that carried me through.

Like the first, this last miscarriage began in the dead of
night. At three in the morning Mike helped me into the
car, and we drove to the hospital. I was struggling to walk
so they brought a wheelchair out for me and took me right
into the ER where a compassionate, young, kind doctor
assured me that the OB on call would be right down.

Mike and I asked her if there were any tests that might
tell us what had happened to the baby. She gently told us
that genetic testing would be possible, and she would make
the arrangements to have it done. Two weeks later we
received the results. The baby had an extremely rare chro-
mosomal disorder called Trisomy 22. The baby's chance of
survival would have been extremely low and would have
been severely physically and mentally disabled. The report
also said that our chances of conceiving another child with
the same disorder were high.

It was time for us to come to terms with the reality that
we might never give birth to a child of our own. It was
time for us to give our hopes for a child to God.

6

The Decision to Adopt

Mike and I never discussed the possibility of "other options" until after my fourth miscarriage. It wasn't until the results of the genetic testing came back that I finally confronted the harsh reality that I might never carry a healthy child to term.

I was intolerable, miserable, inconsolable and unable to feel jubilant for anyone, uncomfortable in my skin. My joy was gone. I was sitting at the kitchen table in our house as the insurmountable pain finally climaxed. I could no longer forge ahead without counseling. I reached over for my pocketbook digging for the number of the social worker that the physician from the last miscarriage had given me. I finally picked up the phone and made the call to schedule an appointment.

As a neurotically prompt person, I arrived fifteen minutes early for my appointment and discovered that the

counselor had her office in hospital's OB/GYN department. The receptionist asked me to take a seat in the waiting room. I sat down among a roomful of pregnant women
struggling not to break down. The minutes seemed like
hours while I desperately tried not to stare at all the large
bellies. Pain was gripping my heart.

Despite the fact that every visit to my counselor meant
sitting in that waiting room with pregnant women, the
time I spent with her filled my vacuum of isolation. Having someone to speak with that was not emotionally connected to me helped me vent all of my frustration and
despair, yet tenderly begin to explore and consider other
options. This was the first stitch in mending the years of
struggle.

In one of our sessions, she gently suggested it might be
time for us to consider those "other" options. The moment
she said it, I had a sudden flashback to seven years earlier,
sitting with my family in the living room of my parent's
house on Cape Cod. My sister was there with her soon to
be husband, and the topic of marriage and children was at
the forefront. I remembered something long buried in my
memory.

I had told everyone, "If I ever discovered that I couldn't
have children, I'd adopt."

It was a memory that set me free. From that moment
on, I was resolute. I never doubted I would someday
become a mother. I knew God had a plan for the creation

of our family—just not the way I thought it would come about.

To ensure we had truly exhausted all of our options, the first thing we did was look for a fertility specialist. After some research, I discovered that the OB/GYN, who had been so sympathetic to me, was now in a practice that dealt with both multiple miscarriages and infertility. I made an appointment for a consultation. When we met with him, he cautioned us that because of the profound genetic abnormality of our last baby, genetic testing had to be part of any plans to have a child and recommended a cutting edge procedure that would involve conception through IVF. I was strongly opposed to the regimen of drugs that were required during the IVF process. Mike and I decided against it.

Next, we considered a surrogate but very quickly dismissed the idea, as it did not resonate very well with either of us. That's when we began seriously to think about adoption. While we had talked about the possibility of adopting a child from another country, it wasn't until a chance conversation with one of my favorite clients that this option came to the forefront. She told me her sister had adopted two boys, eighteen-months and two-years-old, from an orphanage in Siberia. Her story of those two small boys, the challenging conditions in which they had lived, and their new lives in America, was so powerful that I knew I had my confirmation from God.

When I told Mike about my conversation with her and asked what he thought about our trying to adopt a child from an overseas orphanage, his reaction was positive and immediate.

"How do we start?"

So began the eighteen-month journey that led us to our son, Harrison.

7

Harrison's Story

Our son was born in Moldova. Until the summer of 2003, I'd never heard of Moldova, a small country located between Romania and Ukraine that was once part of the former Soviet Union. Mike and I had originally started the paperwork and gathered the documentation needed to adopt a five-year-old boy from Russia, but that had gone terribly wrong. We had learned on New Year's Eve day that the little boy, whose picture I had carried for months, whose clothes and shoes I had already started buying, would not become our son. I didn't think I could bear one more loss or go through the grieving process one more time.

In our bedroom, I dropped to my knees and cried out to Jesus for help. I never blamed Him for the failure of the adoption. I simply continued to lean on Him as He was my only solace.

We began the "document journey" again with more paperwork, more documents and more certifications. Finally, everything was submitted, everything was accepted and we got an email from the agency asking if we would be interested in adopting a seventeen-month-old Moldovan boy named Veaceslav. When we saw the picture attached to the email—he had big blue eyes and an adorable round face—the joy started pouring in again. It seemed that no matter how much loss and disappointment we'd experienced, we could still manage to hope that one day we would have a child of our own.

Three weeks later we were on our way to Moldova, traveling with three other families who were adopting children from local orphanages. One couple had adopted a boy from Russia and was going to Moldova to adopt a little girl. A second couple had previously adopted a son from Moldova and would be adopting another little boy. The third couple was, like us, adopting their first child. They are the most wonderful group of people, and we will be forever connected through the common thread of our children. It was a long, long trip—first to Vienna, then to Romania and from there, to Chişinău, Moldova's capital city. The planes that flew into Moldova were so small (only twenty seats) and cramped that my 6′2″ husband had to bend over to walk down the aisle of the plane. It was so antiquated that I questioned its ability to fly. Mike hates to fly, and he white-knuckled those flights.

At the tiny airport in Chişinău we were met by Doru, a representative from the adoption agency who was there to greet us and drive us to our hotel. Moldova is one of the poorest countries in Europe. This poverty is quite evident when you're driving through the streets. But the people are beautiful. It was the beginning of the school term. Everyone was out walking their children to school—the boys dressed in neat trousers and shirts and the girls in dresses with bows in their hair so big they seemed to cover their entire head. All of them were carrying bouquets of flowers, a traditional gift for their teachers on the first day of class.

We stopped briefly at our hotel—we were all incredibly anxious to see "our" children. We drove out to the orphanage that was located about a ten-minute ride away. It resembled a dilapidated elementary school desperately in need of repairs. The smell of boiling potatoes permeated the air, but the entrance was lined with the most vibrant purple grape vines.

Doru escorted us into what appeared to be a music room with a piano, a large picture of Jesus and His disciples on the wall and invited us to sit down on a row of brightly painted chairs. Moments later, one of the women who cared for the children came into the room carrying a little boy dressed in a green short set.

"This," she said with a big smile, "is Veaceslav."

He looked so small. His skin was almost translucent, and his hair was thin with an odd grayish tint. He had the same big blue eyes and round face we'd seen in his photographs. We had brought animal crackers with us to act as a first meeting icebreaker. He was very shy when we offered him an "elephant." It didn't take long before his face lit up and he reached for another cracker.

After he had finished eating, I held him and carried him around the room, never wanting to let him go. Holding him made all the years of emotional torture just fade away. Then it was Mike's turn. I'll never forget how he fell asleep in Mike's arms with his head resting on Mike's shoulder. He had the face of a sleeping angel.

When he awoke, I selfishly stole him away from Mike—I could not get enough of him. I wanted to try and make him laugh, so I tickled him by crawling my fingers from his legs to his stomach and said, "Tickle, tickle, tickle!" He exploded in a laugh that seemed to come from very deep in his belly. He still has the same deep laugh, and it always takes me back to the first day we met him. There was no question he would become our son.

When Doru came back into the room and asked if we wanted to proceed with the adoption, we, of course, answered, "Yes!"

Then after about forty-five minutes together, it was time to say good-bye. Before the caretaker took Veaceslav back to his room she told him in Romanian, "Give your mother and father a kiss."

Their word for kiss is "poop" so she was telling him to "give us a poop." It was quite comical. I'll always remember her emphasizing, "This is your mother and father." What a gift to finally hear those words.

The next day we were all scheduled to appear before the judge who would decide if the adoption could go forward. I still have the mauve dress I wore that day. I haven't worn it in years as it's woefully out of style, but even though I'm a constant purger of things in my closet, that dress will always be with me.

When Doru arrived to accompany us to court, we all piled in his van which sported a license plate from New Hampshire. I still haven't figured that one out! It was warm and sunny for September, and as we drove through the streets of Chişinău, we were all admiring the beautiful churches with their "onion" domes.

In the courtroom, Mike and I were seated in the front row since we would be the first of the families to appear before the judge. All the other families were asked to leave the courtroom and wait outside. We were left with just Doru, the court stenographer and the woman from social services. He asked fairly general questions.

"What is your name? Why do you want to adopt? Did you see the child? So you want to adopt him? What did you think of him?"

Even though we had an interpreter, I made hand motions I hoped would communicate to the judge that we thought Veaceslav was the most wonderful child in the world and that we would be honored to have him as our son. All my gesturing must have become rather comical, as I saw the court stenographer and the woman from social services trying their best not to laugh.

Finally, the judge left the courtroom to make his decision. He was only gone about ten minutes, but it seemed like an eternity to us. I told Mike it felt as if he'd left for a long European lunch. When he returned with his decision, all I could think was, "*This is it. This is my last chance to have a child.*

We waited anxiously as Doru translated the judge's words, "I have approved the adoption. You are now the parents of Veaceslav Ursu."

Tears of joy flooded my eyes as we thanked the judge and went out into the hallway where the other families were waiting. Seeing my tears, some of them thought we had been rejected, but we shared the good news and hugged each other. As each family came out with the same good news, there were tears of joy all around. The best news of all was that in three short weeks, we could all return to take our children home to the United States.

The moment we returned to Boston, Mike and I started preparing for the arrival of our little boy. We named him Harrison. We'd been in the middle of renovating our house when the call came from the adoption agency, so we had a lot to do in less than a month. When the time came to leave for Moldova, Mike stayed behind to make certain we would, at least, have a functioning kitchen and bathrooms when Harrison arrived—and to build his new son a beautiful wooden swing set.

At the end of September, I reunited with the other adoptive families at Logan Airport in Boston for another sixteen-hour journey to Moldova. We all arrived with our empty baby carriages in tow prepared to board the flight that would forever change our lives. After a night sleepless from excitement in the now familiar hotel in Chişinău, it was off to the orphanage to pick up the children for what I dubbed "Document and Interview Day."

Although the weather was warm, we arrived to find the children dressed for Siberia. Harrison had on two hats and five layers of clothing. But no diaper. The lack of a diaper, I soon realized, was the reason for all those layers of clothes. As I carried Harrison out to the van, I remembered thinking how heavy he was at nineteen pounds and nineteen-months old. He was thin but solid and muscular, which I thought was quite good for a child who had been living in an orphanage with limited means.

We set off for the United States Embassy in Doru's van, which had no seatbelts or car seats. I held Harrison on my lap and watched as he stared intently out the window. *Had he ever been outside the orphanage?*

At the Embassy, waiting our turn for the exit interview required for anyone wishing to adopt a child from Moldova, I sat in a chair and Harrison stood up against a wall, hands touching it, rocking back and forth with a blank stare.

I can't imagine what he must have been thinking. He'd been taken off in a van by a woman speaking a language he did not understand, who he'd been told to call "mother." He was now in a building he'd never seen before, surrounded by more people speaking in that same strange language.

Our interview by an Embassy staffer was quick and informal. We got the paperwork we needed to finalize the adoption, which would take place in Bucharest, Romania. Moldova is so small that many legal matters were still handled in Romania.

After dropping the children off at the orphanage, we set off to various government buildings to sign what seemed like a mountain of documents. At our first stop, Doru left us in the van while he ran inside. When we opened the van door to let in the warm fall breeze, I saw a woman wearing a print shift dress with a babushka tied around her head sitting on the cement steps in front of an apartment house. I decided to take a picture of her—something uniquely "Moldovan" to remember that special day. As I began photographing her, a man waving a gun came charging up to the van screaming in Romanian. I didn't know it, but taking pictures of a public building was prohibited in Moldova. He threatened to take away my camera filled with so many memories, but thankfully, Doru reappeared and managed to straighten everything out.

The photograph I took of that woman is framed and sits on Harrison's dresser. Every time I go into his room and glance at the picture, it takes me right back to that moment—the joy of that day, not the man with the gun!

The following day, all the families packed up in preparation for the trip to Bucharest to finalize the adoptions. At the orphanage I changed Harrison into the new forest green corduroy overalls and the yellow polo shirt I'd brought for him. Everyone was asking us to be quick, to hurry, to move things along, and he began to cry quite loudly. Harrison and I were the last to finish. As we went down the hallway that led to the front door of the orphanage, I noticed a light illuminating our pathway that was shining so brightly I almost closed my eyes. I'd never in my life seen a light shine so brightly, and I knew immediately it was Jesus and thought of Psalm 199:105, "Thy word is a lamp unto my feet, and a light unto my path." Jesus had come walking with us as we began the journey home. In my heart, I knew He was saying, "I told you I would be with you. I told you I would answer your prayers. You will see that I will make up seven times for your pain and grief."

As I write this, Harrison is now a young adult. He loves to read, ski and play golf. He's constantly singing around the house—songs he makes up himself—and is devoted to his dogs, Slavich, a Coton de Tulear and Coco and Mimi, two Yorkshire Terriers. Each year, we celebrate two very important days. On September 2 (the date the judge approved the adoption) we go out to dinner at a restaurant chosen by Harrison. On September 30 (the day we brought him home to Boston) I make a traditional

Moldovan dinner consisting of borscht and other special-ties. I found the recipes in a cookbook purchased for this yearly event. Harrison treasures these anniversaries and looks forward to them each year.

At six, Harrison accepted Jesus as his Savior. I often think of the verse from Jeremiah 1:5, "Before I formed you in the womb I knew you, before you were born I set you apart." I know that God chose Harrison to be our son and gave us the great privilege of becoming his adoptive parents.

Above: Grapevine lined entrance to Harrison's orphanage in Moldova.

Below left: Harrison first met his new Dad and clearly felt comfortable.

Below right: The first day I met Harrison. This is when I started to tickle him and he exploded with a deep belly laugh.

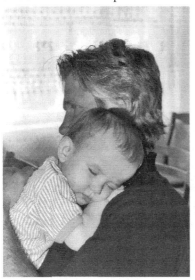

Left: Harrison and me
on our way to the US
Embassy in Moldova
for our interview and
paperwork day.

Right: Harrison's second
day at home in the United
States . . . a happy boy.

Below: Harrison's first night
after leaving the orphanage.
Fast asleep in Bucharest,
Romania where we had to
finalize the adoption.

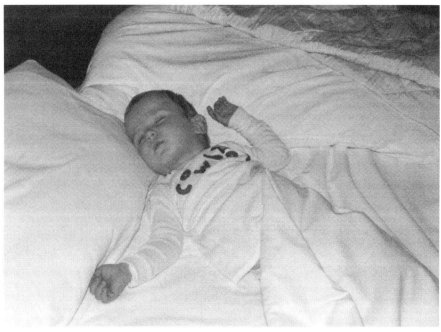

Above: Easter weekend in Martha's Vineyard.

Below: Harrison amongst the Icelandic horses while traveling in Iceland.

Harrison with his two Yorkies, Mimi and Coco.

Christmas Eve in anticipation!

Harrison with my first Icelandic horse, Vaka.

A kiss in Rome, Italy after yet another gelato, one of Harrison's favorite treats!

Above: Lounging on the boardwalk in Florida during Harrison's yearly trip to visit his grandparents.

Right: Harrison on his last day of school with his Dad.

Below: Harrison practicing his putting before his golf tournament.

Harrison, 13 years old, on his first day of school with his three dogs,
Mimi, Coco and Slavich.

BOOK
TWO

Advice for Parents, Family, and Friends

8

Life in a World Full of Children

When I first became pregnant, the world seemed suddenly filled to overflowing with children. There were babies everywhere—on the street outside my office, being pushed in strollers through Home Depot and T.J. Maxx. Normal everyday activities were now seen in the context of my new role as a mother-to-be. When I shopped for groceries, I wheeled my cart down the "baby" aisle, stopping to study the shelves stocked with pureed apricots and rice cereal. When I looked in the paper for movie listings, I checked out which local theaters showed the most G-rated films. If I hit standstill traffic outside a local elementary school I thought, *Someday, I'll be waiting in a line like that to pick-up my child* instead of *What idiot decided to build a school on a busy road.*

Yet after my miscarriages, this happy baby-filled world became fraught with emotional landmines. It seemed as if everyone around me was becoming pregnant and anxious for me to share in their excitement. Events I had always loved, family gatherings and Christmas parties, were now things to be endured if I went at all. Even an innocent question like, "How are you?" could elicit a flood of tears.

I was usually at a loss when it came to handling those emotional land mines. I asked Ellen Clark, LCSW, a clinical counselor at Vanderbilt University, if she could offer some insights and guidance as to how best navigate some of the most common but daunting challenges of living life in a world filled with children.

"In my twenty-three years of practice," said Ellen, "I've counseled so many women who have struggled to recover from the emotional impact of miscarriages. One of the most difficult challenges is living in a culture that doesn't support grief, particularly when it's grieving the loss of a child through miscarriage. Women are expected to return to their everyday lives as if nothing had happened and to function in a world where they're confronted by daily reminders of what they have lost. Because of this, it's important for them to have some practical tools to help them cope with these challenges."

On the following pages I offer some solutions for these difficult situations.

"So How Are You Doing?"

Lori: I had managed to survive Christmas, and when New Year's Eve arrived I thought I was safe. New Year's Eve is, after all, an adult holiday—a celebratory child-free zone.

That afternoon, I decided to drop in at the local nail salon for a quick manicure. As I was sitting in a chair drying my freshly painted red nails, I heard someone calling my name. A longtime friend of my parents came over, planted herself next to me and with a big smile, asked, "How are you?"

It was The Question. The question for which I never seemed to have an answer.

What I wanted to say was, "Horrible, sad, Christmas was agony. I am desperate for a child. It is not happening. I feel out of control," but instead, I once again found myself mumbling,

"Fine, thanks."

Seemingly reassured by my "fine," she began telling me about the plans surrounding the upcoming birth of her grandchild, including a very detailed description of how the nursery had been decorated. She finished with a cheery, "Happy New Year!" and went off to have her nails done. I left the salon feeling crushed and powerless, defeated yet again by a simple, "How are you?"

Ellen: The first thing to consider before you answer is how "safe" is the person who's asking? Is it a close friend, a person you know only casually or someone with a reputation for being insensitive or passing on gossip?

If the question comes from an acquaintance or someone whose motives are suspect, never feel guilty about saying, "I'm fine, thank you" and leaving it at that.

When the question comes from a close friend, you may feel comfortable telling them the truth—that you're still in pain, very sad and working through your grief. Even with good friends, being truthful can open you up to the possibility that their response might be unintentionally thoughtless or hurtful. If you're feeling emotionally fragile, it might be best simply to say, "I'm okay."

If your friend picks up on your sadness and asks again, "Are you *really* okay?" then consider sharing what you're struggling with that day.

It's also important to consider the environment in which the question is being asked. Are you talking to a friend in the check-out line at the grocery store or are the two of you having lunch at her kitchen table? Is it a safe environment in which you feel comfortable having a conversation about your loss? If it's not, "I'm fine," is all you need to say.

Coping with Pregnant Family and Friends

Lori: During the two years I suffered my miscarriages, my sister became pregnant and gave birth to my nephew. I found out about her pregnancy by sheer chance. We had just celebrated my father's 70th birthday with a big party at her home and a number of "thank you for inviting me" cards were displayed on the fireplace mantle in her kitchen. As my sister was cooking dinner, I was idly looking through them when I saw a big "Congratulations!" written at the bottom of one card. Congratulations for what, I thought? Well, being the problem-solver that I am, it didn't take me long to put it together. Lisa was pregnant. My first reaction was anger and a feeling of betrayal. Why hadn't I been one of the first people she told? My family tried to reassure me that they had put off telling me because they "didn't want to hurt me." Keeping the news from me caused greater pain.

Ellen: Friends and family members becoming pregnant while you're still grieving the loss of your child is a situation many women face. Plan ahead and have some automatic responses ready. "I'm so happy for you" or a simple "Congratulations" followed by a hug. You don't have to say more. It's perfectly all right to tell a friend that while you want to be there for her during her pregnancy, right now it's too painful for you. Tell her that as you work through your recovery, you look forward to reconnecting with friends. One word of caution: You can't count on even your best friends telling you about their pregnancy in a way that won't cause you pain. It's important to have someone in your life (a spouse, friend or therapist) you can confide in and with whom you can honestly share your feelings if you've been hurt.

Baby Showers

Lori: I have to admit that I never attended a baby shower during the years of my miscarriages. It was simply more than I could have emotionally handled.

Ellen: Whether to attend a friend's baby shower is a very personal decision, and there is no right or wrong choice. Accepting or declining an invitation should be based on your relationship with her and where you are in your grieving process. If you decide to go, let your friend know that if it becomes too painful, you might not be able to stay. If you do leave early, there's no need to make excuses. Just quietly get up and go. Even when you've decided to decline the invitation, you can still let your friend know you're thinking of her. Why not ask a mutual friend to buy a gift for you and take it with her to the shower?

Holidays

Lori: My sister, Lisa, and I have always enjoyed shopping together during the Christmas holidays. When she called to see if I could join her and my niece, Alexandra, for an evening at a local mall, I readily agreed. Since Lisa had three children to shop for, many of our visits were to kid-friendly stores. I love my nieces and nephews and tried my very best to get into the holiday spirit. By the time we arrived at the Lego store, I could feel myself becoming overwhelmed by thoughts of what I did not have that Christmas—a child of my own.

When our shopping was finished, and it was time for us to say good-bye, I watched as Lisa and Alexandra walked away hand-in-hand—a mother and daughter filled with the joy of the season. Loneliness and emptiness enveloped me more than I could ever have imagined. Even to this day, I'm not able to recount this story without tears.

Ellen: All holidays can be challenging, particularly Thanks-giving and Christmas, as they are so associated with fami-lies and children. Because of this, it's very helpful to have a "plan" for the holidays. Knowing where you will be and what you will be doing (perhaps even hour by hour) will provide a known framework when your emotional world is unpredictable.

Creating a meaningful ritual—lighting a candle and saying a prayer for your baby on Christmas Eve, can help focus and contain some of your pain and may make the holidays feel more survivable.

It's also important that you keep expectations low and the demands on yourself minimal compared to past holi-days. The holidays can be exhausting even for people who are not feeling the emotional weight of grief. Let yourself off the hook and only do what feels comfortable and doable during these times. Take time out to exercise and stay clear of alcohol, high fat and high sugar foods.

Family Get-Togethers

Lori: My family has been going to Hollywood, Florida, since I was five years old. For many years we stayed in a hotel we jokingly described as one step up from camping. It was quite a quirky place with small kitchens in the rooms and appliances that might or might not work on any given day. But we loved it, and it didn't take long for news of our vacation find to spread among my parents' friends and relatives. Before we knew it, fifty exuberant Italians from Boston were taking over the hotel for two weeks every April. As the "children" began having children of their own, we decided it was time for a new place (one where the stoves consistently worked). My sister found a beautiful hotel on the beach that suited all our needs.

I had miscarried for the fourth time in March and my social worker strongly recommended that I not go along for the family's annual trip to Florida. Unfortunately, I did not heed her advice. In Florida, I assured myself, I would be surrounded by the people closest to me and sheltered by a place I had loved since childhood. What could go wrong?

The very first night we were all outside preparing to eat dinner, and all the mothers were tending to their children's needs and preparing their plates. I sat there struggling to eat, practically choking on my food. When I could stand it no longer, I rushed to my room and dissolved in a flood of tears.

Ellen: Even though you love the children in your extended family, being around them can be a painful reminder of your loss. One thing most people don't know is that some of the most sensitive and compassionate responses to grief can come from children—"Are you sad? Can I sit with you until you feel better?"

Opening your heart to the children in your family can be healing for some women but painful for others. Joining in family celebrations is always a personal decision. The best thing to do is honestly communicate your needs so that your family can understand, no matter what your preferences. If you are not comfortable sharing this directly, have your spouse communicate for you—"Sue is still grieving the loss of our baby and needs more time before she can rejoin any family activities/celebrations."

Mother's Day

Lori: I went to church on the Mother's Day following my second miscarriage. As women entered the sanctuary, all the mothers were presented with carnations. During the service, they were asked to stand so the congregation could honor them. I, who had twice been a mother, did not stand. Looking back, I wonder how many other women remained seated that morning because they felt unworthy to claim the title of Mother. Thankfully, my church now recognizes all women on Mother's Day. I proudly stand—not just for Harrison, but also for all our children.

Ellen: This is a tough one. First, do not leave Mother's Day unstructured or unplanned or it will hit you like a ton of bricks. Decide in advance how and with whom you'll be spending the day. Mother's Day is another time when you need to create a ritual such as putting flowers on the altar at church in your child's memory. If you've created a special space or place in memory of your baby—perhaps you've planted a tree or special flower bed in your yard, set aside time to pray or simply sit quietly in that space.

9

Advice for Family and Friends

For the family and friends of a couple who have lost a child to miscarriage, knowing how to respond to their grief can be particularly challenging. While there are familiar words and rituals we can turn to when a spouse, parent or older child has died, we live in a society where miscarriage is regularly dismissed as not being a death; the child not acknowledged as a "real" baby. I hope this chapter will offer practical guidance to friends and family wanting to offer comfort and support to parents grieving a miscarriage.

Words of Comfort That Should Never Be Said

As painful as my first miscarriage was, I was totally unprepared for the emotional pain—the absolute gut wrenching pain—that would come from what I came to call "The Comments."

For some reason, the words of comfort so often heard by parents after a miscarriage are words that do nothing more than increase their grief. If you were comforting a friend whose husband had died unexpectedly, would you ever consider telling her, "It was God's will" or "Don't worry, you'll start dating again and find a new husband"?

If someone you love or simply a friend or acquaintance has suffered the loss of a child, please be conscious that comments such as those listed below—no matter how well-meaning—can pierce an already broken heart.

"It's a blessing. Who knows what might have been wrong with your poor baby."
Pregnancy and giving birth to a child is a blessing. Losing one is not.

"Your baby's an angel in heaven now."
A couple that has lost a child wants their baby to be with them and not in heaven.

"This will make your relationship with God so much stronger."
Everyone has such a personal relationship with God that it's not possible for anyone else (no matter how close the relationship) to truly understand another person's walk with the Lord.

"It's a blessing it had happened before you were really attached to the baby."
Always remember that parents who have lost a child to miscarriage, no matter if it was at six weeks or six months, have already emotionally bonded with and had dreams for that child and their life together.

"My (sister, cousin, friend) had (one, two, three, four) miscarriages and she just had a healthy baby."
Now you've totally terrified your sister, cousin or friend and confirmed her worst fear—that she will have yet another miscarriage.

"You're still young. You have plenty of time." "Don't worry, you'll get pregnant again."
This is a dismissal of what has happened. What you see as "plenty of time," a woman who has suffered a miscarriage often sees as urgency.

"Have you considered adoption, surrogacy or IVF?"
This tells a woman you're assuming she'll never be able to have a successful pregnancy. Each couple has to come to this decision themselves when they are ready and in their due time.

Please, prayerfully consider your words before you speak. For those of you who may have already made an insensitive remark, it's never too late to offer an apology. You have no idea how healing that can be.

The Best Ways for Family and Friends to Offer Their Love and Support

Never underestimate the power of simple words. . . . "I'm so sorry. You're in my prayers" . . . and gestures (a phone call, a card, flowers, a hug, an invitation to dinner) when it comes to healing a broken heart.

Be there to listen—in person, on the phone or by email. A woman who has experienced a miscarriage may need to tell her story repeatedly. Listen patiently. Be sensitive to times when you should remain silent, as sometimes it's best to say nothing at all. Allow her to tell her story without passing judgment.

Don't avoid friends who are grieving the loss of their child, as this makes parents feel that you're not acknowledging their baby's life and the future they had planned for their family.

Don't change the subject when parents talk about the miscarriage. It is often difficult for them to talk openly about the experience, and it's important that friends and family support this part of the healing process.

Make a specific offer of help, not a vague, "Please call if I can do anything for you." Offer to do those everyday things that can seeming overwhelming to a grieving family—do laundry, mow the lawn, run errands, weed the flower beds, drive their children to soccer practice and stay to cheer them on. Volunteer to babysit their other children (or pets) so they can go away for a weekend alone. If you say, "I'll call you on Monday" or "I'll be by tomorrow afternoon," make certain you keep your promise.

If the baby has been given a name, always refer to him or her by name and never as "it."

Remember that dates such as the anniversary of a miscarriage or expected due date may trigger an emotional response. Sending a card or calling them with an invitation to dinner on that night will let them know you've not forgotten their baby.

10

Responding to Hurtful Comments

No matter how loving and supporting your family, friends, and church community are after a miscarriage, you and your husband will, at some point in time, come face to face with a comment or a situation that's so painful it will literally take your breath away. In one of the support groups I attended, we did role-playing—acting out how best we could respond to painful and insensitive comments. I found role-playing to be especially empowering, as I had always retreated into my shell and said nothing at all when anyone (even unintentionally) said something hurtful.

I've put together a list of some of the most often heard comments and then given a suggested response. But use them as a starting point and then craft something in your voice. If you're not up to working out responses on your own, ask a trusted friend or someone in your support group to role-play until you get answers with which you feel comfortable. When you're able to respond in a forthright and kind way (instead of with resentment or bitterness), you'll feel powerful and confident—not a victim or someone to be pitied.

Comment: It's a blessing. Who knows what might have been wrong with the poor baby.
Response: I know that someday we'll understand God's plan, but right now we're still grieving the loss of our child.

Comment: Your baby's an angel in heaven now.
Response: I know you mean well, but what I wanted was to have my baby here with me.

Comment: This will make your relationship with God so much stronger. What do you think God wants you to learn from this experience?"
Response: What I'm learning from this experience is that God's in control of my life and sometimes that can be incredibly painful. My greatest desire in life is to have a child. Right now, it's hard to sit back and let God be in charge.

Comment: It's a blessing it had happened before you were really attached to the baby.

Response: I *was* attached to my baby. From the moment I found out I was pregnant; I began picturing our life together.

Comment: My (sister, neighbor, friend) had (one, two, three, four) miscarriages and she just had a healthy baby.
Response: I understand you're trying to be encouraging, but right now my worst fear is that I might have another miscarriage.

Comment: You're still young. You have plenty of time."
Response: Yes, I'm still young, but we were hoping this would be the time.

Comment: Don't worry, you'll get pregnant again.
Response: We certainly hope so, and we'd be so grateful if you kept us in your prayers.

11

Support Groups

A fter each of my first three miscarriages, I tried to tough it out emotionally on my own. It was an enormous mistake. I talked to Mike, my family and my best friend, Leisa, but as much as they loved me, it was not enough. *Could they ever really understand?* At the time, I didn't know anyone else who had miscarried. It was only later that I discovered several friends and acquaintances had experienced the misfortune of miscarriage, but like me, they had kept silent and never shared their grief.

After my fourth miscarriage, I was truly desperate for help and support. My friends and family were at a loss as to how to comfort me. I looked for a local church that might have a miscarriage support group. Nothing. Finally, my social worker (who had been assigned to me by the hospital after my fourth miscarriage) suggested I join a support group at the Jewish Family & Children's Service. It met on

Tuesday nights and after dinner I raced to get there. It was the time I most looked forward to during the week. The women in the group were from different faiths and backgrounds, but that didn't matter. What did matter was that we could share our grief with others who truly understood our struggle.

Joining the right support group made such a tremendous difference in my journey to healing, but I also remember how difficult it was to find one, even in a big city like Boston. You would assume that all OB/GYN offices and hospitals have a list of local support groups at the ready, but that's not always the case. It's not surprising that a grieving mother won't be up spending hours at the computer or on the phone searching for one. Thankfully, there are national organizations like Share Pregnancy and Infant Loss Support, Inc., that can offer advice and guidance. Share has been helping bereaved families since 1977 and has more than 70 chapters across the United States. They offer peer-to-peer support groups and free information packets as well as a monitored Facebook page, bimonthly newsletter, and blog.

"Some people," says Share Executive Director Cathi Lammert, "are able to find the comfort they need after the loss of a child within their network of family, friends, and clergy. However, after a few weeks have passed, some of this network may not be able to provide the lending ear a mother needs. A support group has members who have experienced the same loss and most times truly understand your feelings. This validates the experience plus gives a mother hope that she can and will get through this difficult time."

Advice from Cathi

Don't expect to know if a support group is right for you until you've attended at least two meetings. The first meeting may be filled with just getting used to the place, the members, and the idea of support and you might not find your comfort zone until you've attended several meetings.

Don't worry if you're not a talker. Some people benefit from simply listening to the other members' experiences.

Don't worry if you find that a group dynamic is not for you—some women find their best support comes from working with a professional counselor or one-on-one with the support group leader.

Online support groups can provide a safety net to a grieving mother. The greatest benefit of online groups is that you can post or read messages twenty-four hours a day and these postings and messages are often responded to within the same day by other members and/or facilitators. Make certain you choose a group that is monitored by trained facilitators and *only* accessible through user names and passwords. Be very wary of online groups that are not monitored, as they may be open to hurtful comments from anyone surfing the net.

Starting a Support Group at Your Church

I have to be honest and say that too few churches are providing care and support for those in their congregations and communities who have suffered a miscarriage. While there are support groups for single parents, the recently divorced and those struggling with addiction, miscarriage rarely appears on a church's outreach radar. Many times, it's simply because the pastoral staff has no idea how many couples have been affected. If you told them that the American Pregnancy Association estimates that 10-25% of all pregnancies will end in miscarriage each year, I'm certain they would be staggered by the number.

One of the most important steps in my healing journey was finding the courage to reach out and share my experience with others. When you're at a point in your journey that you too can begin to reach out, consider speaking with your pastor about starting a miscarriage support group in your church. For inspiration, I've included the stories of two such ministries and the women who gave them life.

Traders Point Christian Church is a non-denominational church with locations in Indianapolis, Carmel, and Whitestown, Indiana. Their Heart to Heart Ministry offers comfort, encouragement and resources to those who have lost a child to ectopic pregnancy, stillbirth, miscarriage or early infant death. It began, as do many ministries, with a searching heart.

"I'd been looking for an outreach I could really become involved in," remembers Jenny Parker, "and one Sunday as I was walking into the service a Senior Pastor stopped me and shared his concern for couples in the congregation who were struggling with the loss of a child."

As Jenny was a Licensed Clinical Social Worker who had suffered a miscarriage of her own, he hoped she would be interested in creating a ministry that would reach out to help these grieving parents.

Jenny began by praying and talking with the church's counseling minister. He suggested she contact Marti Sorgen, who had lost a child shortly after birth and Barb Baxter, who had suffered three miscarriages.

"The three of us," says Jenny, "had been strangers up until then, but we got together, shared our stories with one another, cried and encouraged each other. When it came to setting a direction for the ministry, we focused on one thing—when we went through our losses, what did we need that wasn't there for us?"

The first thing they did was create a binder that included Bible verses, poems, a cassette (now a CD) of their testimonies and a resource list of books and Christian pregnancy loss websites. Because they felt it was essential to include "something tangible to show that the little person had actually existed," they included an In Remembrance of Our Baby certificate that could be filled out by the parents and a small gold cross pin.

The ministry had its official launch in December 2000 at a Sunday morning service.

"A friend sang "I Am Not Alone" by Natalie Grant, and the three of us had a brief time to talk about our hopes for Heart to Heart. For several weeks after that, we set up a table outside the sanctuary where we handed out our binders and answered questions. We had women come up in tears and want to tell their stories and friends or family members stop by asking how they could best help a loved one struggling with the loss of a child.

When we put an announcement of the first meeting of a Heart to Heart group in the bulletin, there was no response. Not one. I had people run away from me when I mentioned joining the group. I began to think we had seriously misunderstood what God's plan was for the ministry.

Within a few months, a woman who had visited the church asked Jenny if she would consider leading a group of eight women (none of whom attended Trader's Point) who would meet at her home. The group met for nine weeks using Shari Bridgman's book *In Heavenly Arms: Grieving the Loss, Healing the Wounds of Miscarriage* as an informal guide.

"What that experience taught us," says Jenny, "was that in the case of Heart to Heart we didn't need to try—God would tell us when it was time for a group to form and who would comprise that group."

In the years since, all the Heart to Heart groups have been brought together by God's leading.

"One group had just two couples; sometimes it was just the ladies. When it's women only, we always ask the husbands to join us when we discussed how men and women grieve differently. Groups typically run from eight to nine weeks, but if a group needs to spend time on something like the grieving process we take all the time needed. It's so important to be very flexible. We do maintain a structure, but we let the group guide us as to how much time we spend on each topic."

"Initially, this ministry was as much for our own healing as it was for reaching out to others. Deep friendships have grown from the experience of developing the ministry. Our resource packets have gone out all over the United States, and I have talked personally to so many women needing encouragement and a listening ear. I have been tremendously blessed to minister to others who are suffering the pain I experienced losing a child. It has strengthened my faith in the healing power of God and in His ability to use our pain to grow us and make us more compassionate toward others."

North Parkersburg Baptist Church is a multi-generational church located in Parkersburg, West Virginia. The Our Hope Ministry began, remembers its founder, Ronni Edmands,

> ". . . as an idea placed in my heart by God. My husband
> and I had been struggling with infertility for a few
> years, and I felt so alone as if there was no one who

understood what I was going through. Even though it
seemed as if everyone I knew was having babies, I knew
there must be others just like me in the community
who were trying to work through the pain of a miscarriage and infertility. Like me, they were trying to do
it alone."

With the blessing of Pastor Kent Boone, Ronni
reserved a space at the church and began letting the community know about the new Our Hope Ministry. Their
mission was to encourage one another, share medical
resources and information, pray for and be there for one
another. Ronni found that "simple word of mouth was the
most effective way to get the word out, as many women
who are dealing with a miscarriage or infertility know of
another woman who shares that struggle."

She also sent out mailings to area churches and counsel-
ors announcing the ministry and printed up Our Hope
Ministry business cards, showing the dates and times of
scheduled meetings, Ronni's name and phone number and
the church's website. She distributed them to local OB/
GYN and family medicine practices.

The first meeting was held in January, 2006.

"There were five of us," says Ronni, "and none of this
initial group were members of the church. They all came
from our get-the-word-out campaign. We sat in a circle,
feeling a little awkward but so thankful we had connected
with others who could listen and understand. We shared a

little about ourselves and what had brought us to Our Hope. We ended the first session with a prayer that God would heal our bodies and hearts."

Our Hope soon grew to a series of monthly meetings. Ronni had no formal lesson plans for the meetings, ". . . We did everything from sharing and drawing questions out of a jar ("How has this impacted you spiritually?" or "What does suffering mean to you?") to role playing on how to best deal with insensitive comments."

They also invited other women to come and share their stories. One of the most memorable for the group was Lisa Welch, a missionary from Africa who had lost a child one day before her due date.

"Lisa was an inspiration to all of us because, despite her devastating loss, she remained hopeful that God would bless her with a child. She turned the loss of her daughter into a ministry to help others experiencing infertility and pregnancy loss."

By 2008, the nature of the ministry had evolved from small group meetings to its current outreach that pairs women who are experiencing early pregnancy loss or infertility with a prayer partner who has faced similar struggles.

"The women from Our Hope pray for them and offer informal counseling. We always give the women options—some are very private and their story goes no further than my ears. Others want as much support as possible and enjoy meeting their prayer partners for lunches and being part of a prayer group."

For Ronni, the years since the beginning of Our Hope have brought both joy and pain.

"We underwent a wide variety of treatments for infertility including in vitro which resulted in the birth of our twins, Andrew and Kayte. I had been pregnant with triplets and lost our third baby in the first trimester. We also experienced a failed adoption before God led us back to in-vitro. My involvement with Our Hope has grown me both spiritually and emotionally. I've seen God answer the prayers of so many women—perhaps not the answers we anticipated, but always answers that reflected God's glory."

12

Remembering Your Baby

Miscarriage is still the Silent Loss; the death rarely acknowledged. Parents who have lost a child to miscarriage are all too often expected to go quietly on with their lives and never speak of "it" again. Honoring your baby's life, in a way that's meaningful to you, is an important part of healing.

- Plant a tree or donate a swing set in your baby's name to a local park.
- Create a memorial garden in your yard. Flowers such as marigolds, cosmos and zinnias will attract butterflies, which are often seen as a symbol of comfort for grieving parents.
- Engrave a Christmas ornament with the date of your baby's birth.

- Donate to a local charity that has an outreach to young children.
- Schedule a yearly memorial service for all parents who have lost children to miscarriage.
- Place flowers on the altar on the anniversary of your baby's death. Work with your pastor to make certain that the Mother's Day service honors all women— including those who have lost a child to miscarriage.
- Hold a memorial service to honor your baby. This can be a simple service held in your home with only a few close family and friends or a service at your church that would include friends from work and the congregation.

While the details of any memorial service should minister to the needs of each congregation and community, Jenny Parker, co-founder of the Heart to Heart Ministry at Traders Point Christian Church in Whitestown, Indiana, was kind enough to share a brief overview of the annual service held at Traders Point.

> The service is open to everyone in the community, is announced on local Christian radio and in a mailing to fifty local churches. We begin with praise and worship featuring two guitarists and two vocalists, and after everyone is welcomed, we have a reading that includes the lighting of candles in remembrance of our babies. Two poems are then recited (one written by a member of our first miscarriage support group), and a soloist sings

"Glory Baby" by Enya on her album *Watermark*. A message given by one of our pastors is followed by a video of the song "He Knows My Name" and a recitation of the poem "Hope" by Chera Correnti. We finish with a soloist singing "With Hope" by Steven Curtis Chapman. I usually close the service with a reading of Romans 15:13, "May the God of hope fill you with all joy and peace as you trust in him, so that you may overflow with hope by the power of the Holy Spirit" and an invitation to parents to write a note to their child and join us outside, where we attach the notes to balloons and launch them toward Heaven.

Most importantly, honor the memory of your child by sharing (when you are able) your journey with others. The help and support that comes from someone who has traveled the same painful road is invaluable.

Moving On:
Finding a Passion for Living

The memory of your loss will always be there. The pain may never go away. It's so important for your healing that you ease that pain with something that will make you smile and give you great joy. I know the thought of seeking out joy when your heart is still raw may seem a betrayal of your child and their loss, but embracing a passion can change your life in ways you can never begin to imagine. Your passion may be something you've done for years but put aside because it seemed incompatible with your grief.

Or it may be something entirely new—something you've always had a million excuses for not trying.

My passion is horses, but I have friends who have used their love for running, tennis, skiing, golf and knitting see them through the darkest of times. No matter what you choose, the most important thing is that you never let yourself fall into the trap of saying, "I don't have time for this. I should be focusing on my husband, my job, my other children" or "How can I play tennis when I should be grieving? What will people think?" You are not selfish. This is a time when you absolutely must nurture yourself. It's a time when you have to get up and get moving. You don't know who or what God may put in your path once you set your life back in motion.

Moving On: Lori's Story

During the years between my first and fourth miscarriages, the barn where I boarded my horse was one of the few places where my thoughts were not focused on having a child. At the barn, my friends and I talked about horses and horses and more horses. No one talked about their kids. At that point in my life, I desperately needed a way to not only physically release all my pent up emotions but a way to emotionally escape, if only for a few hours, from my childless reality.

In the dark months after my first miscarriage, I began riding on Monday and Wednesday afternoons with my best friend, Leisa. I leased a small white horse that was aptly named Noble, as he was strong, husky and looked like the horses you see in all the fairy tales. Simply being able to go out into the woods and ride helped heal my grieving heart. Noble gave me something I could take care of, something for which I was responsible, something I could love absolutely.

Even the cold last days of a New England winter couldn't keep me from the barn after my second miscarriage. I loved the winter rides Noble and I took with Leisa and her horse—especially if we were lucky enough to ride when snow had just fallen. We'd return to the barn just before dusk. After seeing that the horses were settled for the night, Leisa and I would huddle in the barn's only heated room with the wine and cheese we'd brought from home, talking and laughing about the day's ride. Those times, spent in a tiny room with a once in a lifetime friend, gave me the comfort and strength I needed to face my childless home.

Summer rides in the Blue Hills Reservation outside of Boston emotionally sustained me after my third miscarriage. Leisa and I would ride along the miles of wooded trails, around ponds and through big, open meadows. One day, as we were feeding our usual need for speed, we found ourselves galloping back and forth through a field laughing hysterically. Hysterical laughter—the kind that causes pain to your stomach muscles, is by far the best "medicine." Back at the barn, we decided the afternoon was too beautiful to head home, so we grabbed a blanket from the car and parked ourselves on the ground near the paddocks where we could see all the horses. We sat there with friends from the barn and laughed again as we thought about the two of us galloping like crazy teenagers. It was the laughter that I cherished most during those times.

After my fourth miscarriage, I decided it was time to buy my dream horse. Three months later, I found Vaka, a pinto Icelandic mare with a long black and white mane and a soft, gentle eye. The moment I saw Vaka, I knew immediately that she was the one.

On the day she was due to arrive at the barn, I was so excited I headed to the barn a full two hours early to meet her. Leisa came with me, camera in hand, to share the moment. Finally, I saw Bunny, the driver, pulling in with Vaka. When she unloaded her into my hands, I knew a new chapter in my life was about to begin.

The Saturday after Vaka arrived, nothing could have kept me from the barn. It was a beautiful crisp, early autumn day, and the leaves were just starting to change colors, the perfect day to introduce Vaka to the Blue Hills. We headed out alone and meandered down a quiet road before we crossed into the entrance of our usual trail in the Blue Hills.

Vaka was cooperative and brave. When we arrived at a crossroad, I decided to take the path down a fairly steep hill lined with intensely colored trees. I stopped at the bottom of the hill to absorb the peace and beauty that surrounded me. The silence was broken by the sound of an owl.

I looked up to see a stunning Snowy Owl in the trees. I happily tucked this away as a sign that life was moving in the right direction for me. I believe that God is continually showing us signs throughout our day, and we must open our hearts and our minds to recognize those and know He is with us.

My passion for horses has taken me, a city girl, to a new life on Four Winds Farm south of Boston, where Mike and I raise, breed and train Icelandic horses. I ride almost every morning and regularly participate in Icelandic sports competitions. Horses continue to fill my heart with joy and enrich my life in ways too numerous to count.